I0762398

Favorite Favorite

Written by M.H. Clark | Illustrated by Daisy Hirst

My favorite favorite hug is yours,
my favorite favorite face.
And wherever you are
is just my favorite favorite place.

My favorite favorite ice cream
is whatever we can share.

The flavor doesn't matter
just as long as you are there.

My favorite favorite colors
are the ones you like to use.
My favorite favorite songs to sing
are all the ones you choose.

e-i-e-i-o!

My favorite loud, my favorite bright,

my favorite quiet,
cozy night...

My very favorite kind of weather...

is the kind we're in together.

My favorite favorite place to be
is right here next to you.
It's more about your company
than what we choose to do.

My favorite favorite smile of all
just happens to be yours.
I can't think of a single smile
that makes *me* smile more.

My favorite no,

my favorite yes,

my favorite wild and joyful mess...

My favorite oopses and mistakes
are all the ones I watch you make.

My very very favorite we
starts with a you...

and adds a me.

You have my favorite favorite voice,
my favorite favorite laugh.
My favorite favorite questions
are the ones you like to ask.

My favorite up

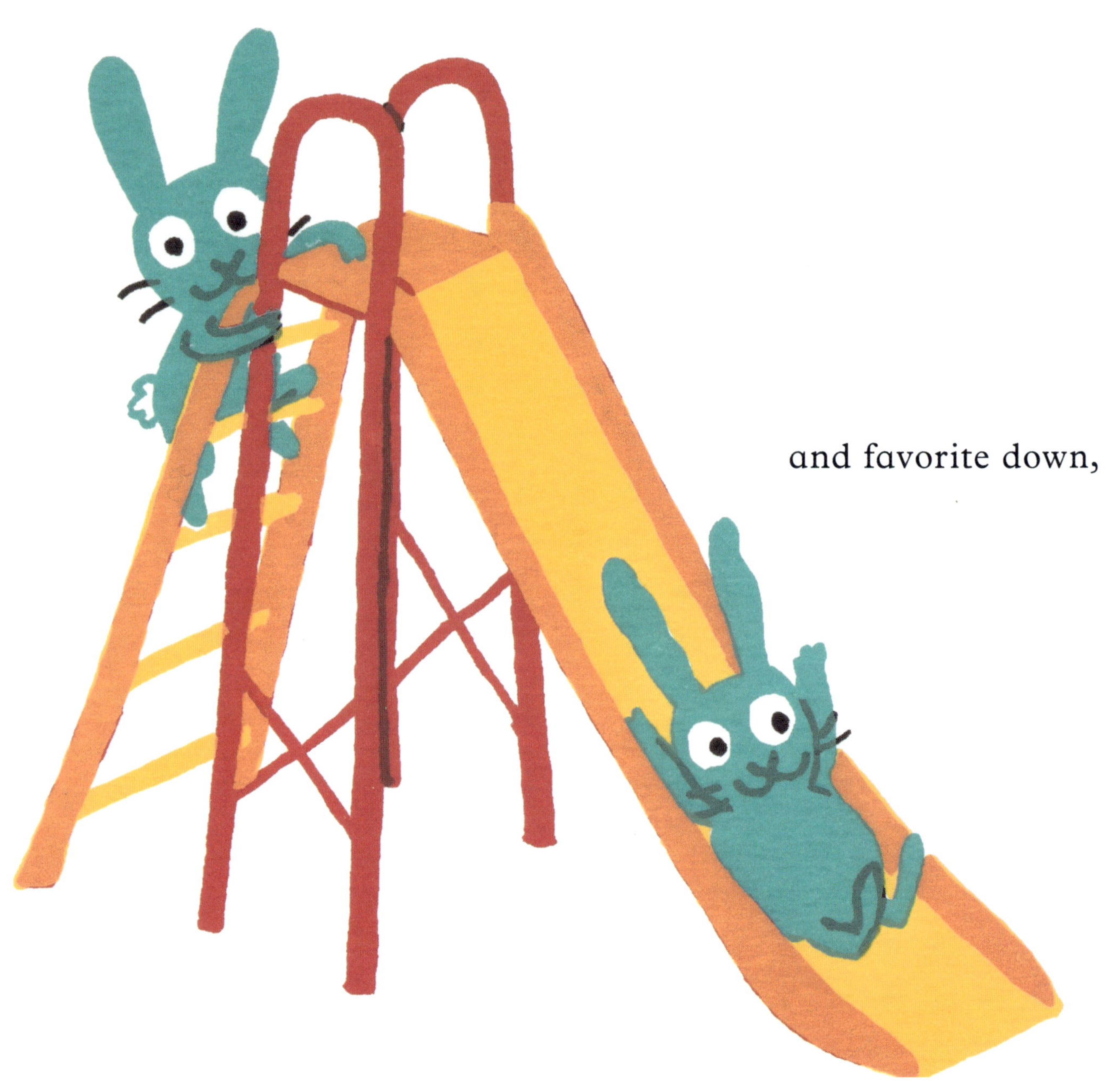

and favorite down,

my favorite bouncing all around.

My favorite can't-make-up-my-mind
is yours, of course. (Yes, every time.)

I've never met another person
all that much like you.

Which makes you very rare, you know,
and that's my favorite too.

And when I think I couldn't have
a single favorite more,
you show me something new about you—
something I adore.

Who else could make the world
so big and brilliant every day?
Who else could find each tiny wonder
all along the way?

Who else could be my very favorite favorite, through and through?
The answer's just so clear to me. The answer's...

only YOU.

An imprint of the Crown Publishing Group
A division of Penguin Random House LLC
1745 Broadway, New York, NY 10019
live-inspired.com | penguinrandomhouse.com

Library of Congress Control Number: 2024948170 | ISBN: 978-1-957891-72-9 | CPSIA: A012510001

Writer: M.H. Clark
Illustrator: Daisy Hirst
Editor: Amelia Riedler
Art Director: Megan Gandt
Production Manager: Olivia Holmes

1st printing. Manufactured in China with soy inks on FSC®-Mix certified paper.

The authorized representative in the EU for product safety and compliance is Penguin Random House Ireland, Morrison Chambers, 32 Nassau Street, Dublin D02 YH68, Ireland, https://eu-contact.penguin.ie.